W9-BAT-402

DYNAMIC PLANET

Exploring Changes on Earth with
SCIENCE PROJECTS

by Tammy Enz

Consultant:
Ginger L. Schmid, PhD, Associate Professor
Department of Geography
Minnesota State University, Mankato

CAPSTONE PRESS
a capstone imprint

Fact Finders Books are published by Capstone Press,
1710 Roe Crest Drive, North Mankato, Minnesota 56003
www.capstonepub.com

Library of Congress Cataloging-in-Publication Data
Enz, Tammy, author.
  Dynamic planet : exploring changes on Earth with science projects / by Tammy Enz.
      pages cm.—(Fact finders. Discover Earth science)
  Summary: "Illustrated instructions for experiments pertaining to changes on Earth,
including plate tectonics, erosion, the greenhouse effect, and glaciers"—Provided by
publisher.
  Includes bibliographical references and index.
  ISBN 978-1-4914-4815-1 (library binding)
  ISBN 978-1-4914-4914-1 (eBook PDF)
1. Earth sciences—Experiments—Juvenile literature. 2. Geology—Experiments—
Juvenile literature. 3. Science projects—Juvenile literature. 4. Earth (Planet)—
Experiments—Juvenile literature. I. Title.
  QE29.E59 2016
  551.078—dc23   2014050240

Editorial Credits
Alesha Sullivan, editor; Sarah Bennett, designer; Kelly Garvin, media researcher;
Lori Barbeau, production specialist

Photo Credits
Capstone Press/Karon Dubke, 8, 12, 13, 15, 18, 19, 21, 24, 28, 29; Shutterstock: beboy,
cover, Budkov Denis, 6, daulon, 11, (bottom), 25 (inset), DavidMurk, 6 (inset), Designua,
9, Dmitry Naumov, 4-5, Doczky, 25, Igor Zh., 14, ixpert, 22-23, hans engbers, 16-17,
Juancat, 7, Kingarion, 23 (bottom right), meunierd, 26-27, Tami Freed, 20, Wead, 10-11

Design Elements: Shutterstock: Curly Pat, Magnia, Markovka, Ms.Moloko, Orfeev,
pockygallery, Sashatigar

Printed in the United States of America in Stevens Point, Wisconsin .
032015   008824WZF15

Table of Contents

Our Lively Planet 4

Experiment 1
Quakes, Oh My! 6

Experiment 2
Plugged Up Magma 10

Experiment 3
Tidal Waves 14

Experiment 4
Wearing Away the Shores 16

Experiment 5
Freezing and Thawing Land 20

Experiment 6
A Gassy Place 22

Experiment 7
Icy Landscape 26

Glossary 30
Read More 31
Internet Sites 31
Index 32

Our Lively Planet

Many people think Earth is solid and unchanging. But it is constantly, often violently, changing. The solid ground we stand on is really a thin crust. Far beneath it Earth's core is intensely hot. Its heat melts parts of the rocky **mantle** below the crust. This **molten** material, pushing through the crust, causes quakes and massive eruptions. Earthquakes, volcanoes, and underwater eruptions continually shape and change Earth's surface and shorelines.

Changes in weather and climate also alter **landscapes** and **biological** systems on our planet. Changing temperatures, rushing water, and creeping glaciers have amazing Earth-changing powers.

Want a close-up look at how Earth changes? Would you like to re-create some of the amazing processes? With a few simple supplies, you can build your own miniature Earth-shattering projects. Some of these experiments may require an adult's help. Think safety first! And remember, science can sometimes be messy—so don't forget to clean up when you're done.

mantle–the layer of hot rock that surrounds Earth's core

molten–melted by heat; lava is molten rock

landscape–the form of the land in a particular area

biology–having to do with plant and animal life

5

Quakes, Oh My!

Earth's surface is a thin rocky crust only about 25 miles (40 kilometers) thick on average. The crust is made of rocky plates. The plates float on a semimolten crust. **Magma** seeps, oozes, and erupts between plate edges.

As plate edges collide, their impact shakes the ground, causing earthquakes. As plates move apart, magma rises to form new landmasses and volcanic eruptions. If an earthquake or volcano happens on the ocean floor, a **tsunami** may be the result.

The theory of **plate tectonics** describes the movement of Earth's plates and the reshaping of Earth's surface. Try this simple yummy project to see plate tectonics in action.

magma—melted rock found beneath the surface of Earth

tsunami—a large, destructive wave caused by an underwater earthquake or volcano

plate tectonics—the scientific theory that the Earth's surface is made of large plates that move very slowly

Growing Discovery

A new island, named Niijima, was discovered in Japanese waters on November 20, 2013. Over the next few weeks, volcanic action caused the island to quickly swell in size. The small island has continued expanding, overtaking a larger island nearby. Niijima has grown to more than 3,280 feet (1,000 meters) across.

What You Do

1. Use the spoon to scoop the frosting into the cake pan. Smooth it out evenly across the bottom of the pan with a spatula.

2. Place the crackers in a single layer over the frosting. Cover the entire surface, making sure not to overlap the cracker edges.

3. With your finger move a cracker in any direction. What happens to the crackers around it and to the frosting below?

4. Using slightly more force, push several crackers together.

What happened when some of the graham cracker "plates" moved away from each other? What do you think will happen if the "magma" frosting is exposed? In real life, when molten material bubbles up to the surface, it is called lava.

What You Need

spoon

container of frosting or marshmallow cream (red food coloring is optional)

cake pan

spatula

package of graham crackers

Theory of Plate Tectonics

Have you ever noticed how Earth's continents look as if they could fit together like pieces of a puzzle? Scientist Alfred Wegener theorized in 1915 that at one time all continents were part of a single landmass. He called this landmass Pangaea, meaning "all the lands." Wegener couldn't explain how the continents drifted apart. But later scientists found support for Wegener's theory. When studying ocean ridges, they found lava spewing from the ocean floor. Over millions of years this action is responsible for pushing plates apart.

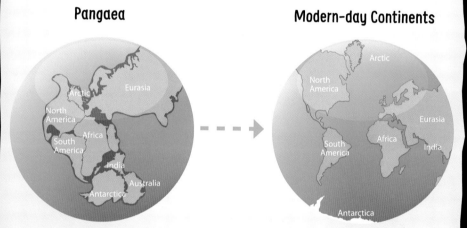

Pangaea

Modern-day Continents

lava—the hot, liquid rock that pours out of a volcano when it erupts; lava is magma that reaches Earth's surface

Plugged Up Magma

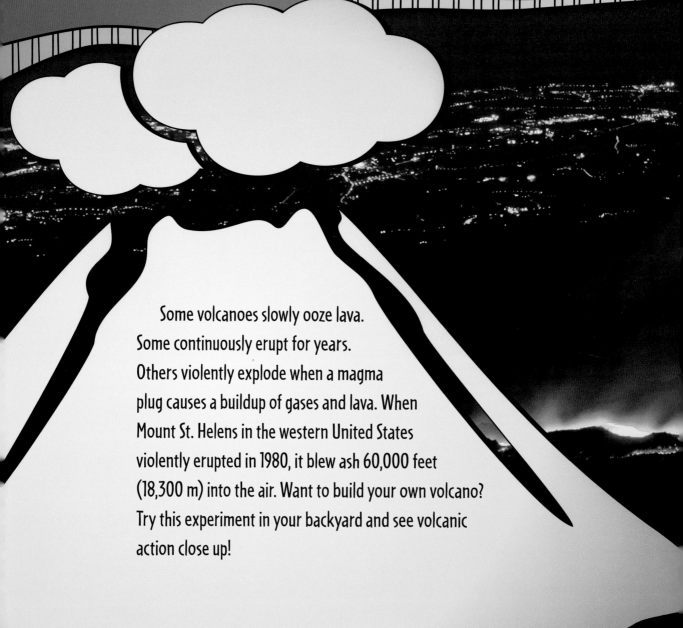

Some volcanoes slowly ooze lava. Some continuously erupt for years. Others violently explode when a magma plug causes a buildup of gases and lava. When Mount St. Helens in the western United States violently erupted in 1980, it blew ash 60,000 feet (18,300 m) into the air. Want to build your own volcano? Try this experiment in your backyard and see volcanic action close up!

As one plate slips below another, the grinding together of the plates produces earthquakes. Plate movement also causes magma to surface.

What You Do

What You Need

empty 2-liter soda bottle

half of a raw potato

towel

white vinegar

baking soda

three squares of toilet tissue

1. Remove the cap from the empty soda bottle.

2. Make a cork by pushing and twisting the cut side of the potato onto the opening of the bottle. Push the potato onto the bottle about 2 inches (5 centimeters). Carefully remove the potato cork, and set aside.

3. Place a towel on an outdoor table and set the bottle in the middle of the towel.

4. Pour 2 cups (480 milliliters) white vinegar into the bottle.

5. Place 1 teaspoon (5 grams) baking soda on the center of each toilet tissue square. Roll the tissue around the baking soda. Twist the ends to form a small packet.

12

6. Drop the baking soda packets into the bottle. Quickly put the potato cork on the bottle, and take several steps away from the bottle. What happened inside and outside of the bottle? What happened to the potato cork? Does the explosion remind you of a volcano?

Safety First!

Because of the force of the explosion, this experiment should be done outside and with adult supervision.

Major Destruction

The most destructive volcano in recorded history was Mount Tambora in Indonesia in 1815. Continuously erupting for months, the volcano killed 90,000 people. The ash it spewed blocked the sun, and the blockage changed Earth's climate. Thousands of miles away, Americans experienced midsummer snow and crop losses. Nonstop rain in Ireland and Great Britain led to crop failure, starvation, and illness.

Tidal Waves

Volcanoes and earthquakes that happen under the ocean cause different effects than those that occur on land. The underwater disruptions can cause tsunamis that crash into shorelines and cause major damage. On average, two destructive tsunamis occur each year worldwide. See for yourself how tsunamis work.

FACT

Tsunamis can travel up to 500 miles (800 km) per hour in deep ocean waters. The waves are about 3 feet (1 m) high. Tsunamis slow down as they approach land, and the waves get bigger. Some waves can reach up to 50 feet (15 m) high!

What You Do

What You Need

sand

plastic container measuring 12 by 24 inches (30 by 60 cm) and at least 6 inches (15 cm) deep

water

3 or 4 small plastic houses and trees

1. Use the sand to build a mini beach about 2 inches (5 cm) high along one end of the plastic container. The beach should extend across about one-quarter of the container.

2. Slowly pour water into the container opposite the beach until the water measures 1 inch (2.5 cm) high.

3. Place the plastic trees and houses on the beach.

4. Gently blow on the surface of the water to create waves.

5. After creating some normal waves, grab the end of the container opposite the beach. Quickly jerk the box toward you. What happened to the trees and houses? Where did some of the sand move?

15

Wearing Away the Shores

Tsunami waves carry beach sand out into the water away from the shore. But the everyday movement of water can also drastically eat away at landmasses. **Erosion** along rivers and shores moves soil from one place to another, which greatly changes the landscape over time. Build your own shoreline and see erosion at work with this experiment.

Caution: This is a messy project and should be done outside.

erosion—the wearing away of land by water or wind

What You Do

What You Need

disposable aluminum cake pan

ruler

marker

utility or craft knife

damp sand

handful of gravel or small rocks

small block of wood

bottle of water

1. In the middle of one side of the cake pan, measure and mark a ½ inch (1.25 cm) diameter circle. The circle should be as close to the bottom of the pan as possible. Use the utility knife to cut out the circle.

2. Spread damp sand in the bottom of the pan about 1 inch (2.5 cm) high.

3. Use your fingers to dig a winding "river bed" in the sand from the hole to the other side of the pan. Your river should be about 1 inch (2.5 cm) wide. Smooth and firm up the banks on both sides of the river.

4. Place several rocks along one of the bends in the river. Place several more along another bend.

5. Prop up the end of the pan opposite the hole on the block of wood.

Helpful Hint: You may need to place the pan on a flat board or book for stability.

6. Slowly pour the water into the riverbed from the propped end of the pan. What happened to the river's shoreline? Where is the **sediment** being carried? How do rocks along the river bends affect erosion?

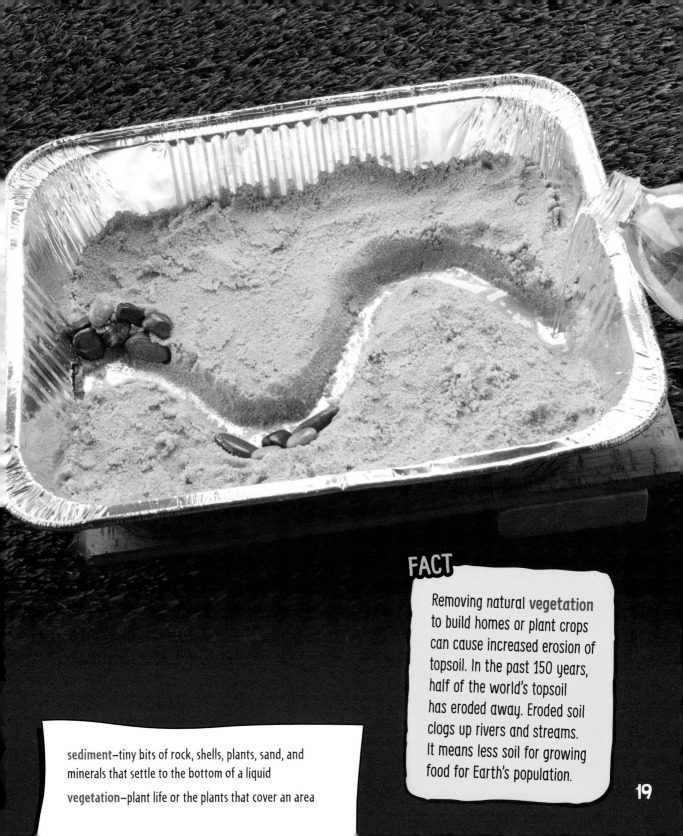

sediment–tiny bits of rock, shells, plants, sand, and minerals that settle to the bottom of a liquid

vegetation–plant life or the plants that cover an area

19

Freezing and Thawing Land

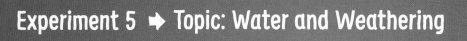

Believe it or not, resting water can change a landscape. Water expands when it freezes, so water can break large rocks apart. Water works its way into small cracks. When the water freezes it opens the cracks. Over a very long time, **weathering** caused by freezing and thawing can turn a mountain into a pile of gravel. Get an inside look at freezing and thawing using a few simple supplies.

FACT

The Appalachian Mountains in North America are considered old, eroding mountains. This range loses about 1/16 of an inch (2 millimeters) in height every hundred years.

weathering—breaking down of solid rock into smaller and smaller pieces by wind, water, glaciers, or plant roots

What You Do

1. Fill a balloon with water until it starts to expand. Tie the balloon shut.

2. Measure and pour ½ cup (114 grams) plaster of paris and ⅓ cup (80 mL) water into the bowl. Stir with a plastic spoon.

Helpful Hint: Do not wash the spoon or bowl used to mix plaster in the sink. The plaster can harden inside the drain and cause damage.

3. Place the balloon into the plaster mixture in the bowl. Roll the balloon around until it is completely covered in plaster.

4. Let the plaster harden around the balloon inside the bowl for 30 minutes. When the plaster has hardened, place the bowl in the freezer.

5. Wait at least one hour before removing the bowl from the freezer. What happened to the plaster?

A Gassy Place

Gases in Earth's **atmosphere** change our planet's surface over time. Earth is like a giant greenhouse. Gardeners use greenhouses to grow plants in cool weather. The glass or plastic buildings allow the sun's heat inside. The plants and ground inside the greenhouse warm up and give off **infrared rays**. But the rays can't escape back outside through the glass building. The rays bounce around and keep the greenhouse warm.

In the same way, the sun's heat warms Earth. When the heat bounces back into space, gases in the atmosphere trap some of the heat. Without the gases Earth would be too cold. But too much of the gases can cause the planet to heat up. Now you can check out how the greenhouse effect works.

atmosphere–the mixture of gases that surrounds Earth

infrared rays–heat rays; a form of radiation similar to visible light that is given off by all warm objects

22

A greenhouse allows the sun's short waves in, but it traps infrared waves to stay warm.

What You Do

1. Pour 2 cups (480 mL) water into each of the jars. Put three ice cubes in each of the jars. Put the lids onto the jars.

2. Put one of the jars inside the clear storage bag, and seal it.

3. Put both jars in a sunny place for an hour.

4. Use a thermometer to measure the temperature of the water inside each jar. What do you notice? Which jar's water reached a higher temperature?

What You Need

cold water

2 medium-sized jars with lids

ice cubes

large, clear storage bag

clock or timer

thermometer

Earth's Rising Temperatures

Scientists have been tracking Earth's average temperatures since the 1880s. Although Earth has gone through several warming and cooling cycles, it has warmed by about 1 degree Fahrenheit (0.5 degrees Celsius) in that time. The levels of **carbon dioxide**, a greenhouse gas, have also increased. Too much carbon dioxide gas released by cars and factories cause Earth to hold on to too much heat. The increase makes the planet warmer and concerns scientists about Earth's future.

carbon dioxide—colorless, odorless gas that people and animals breathe out

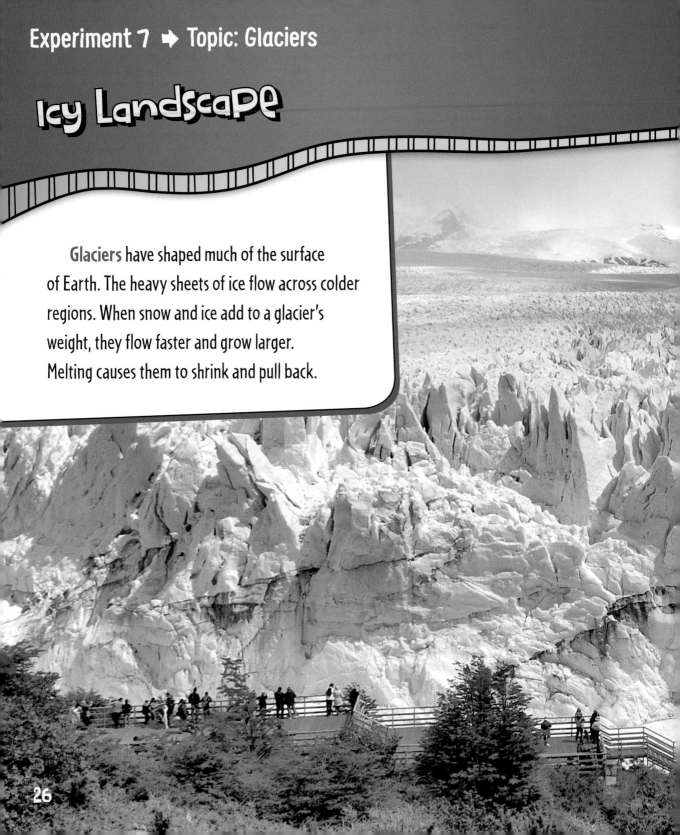

Icy Landscape

Glaciers have shaped much of the surface of Earth. The heavy sheets of ice flow across colder regions. When snow and ice add to a glacier's weight, they flow faster and grow larger. Melting causes them to shrink and pull back.

The moving ice sheets shove piles of rock into hills. They can also carve out deep valleys. Glaciers once covered a majority of Earth's surface. They are still at work in many places. Change up your own landscape with this fun glacier project!

glacier—a huge moving body of ice found in mountain valleys or polar regions

What You Do

What You Need

sand

small pebbles and stones

cake pan

notebook and pencil

books

ruler

2 full 4-ounce (118 mL) bottles
white school glue

2 bowls

warm water

2 spoons

measuring cup

borax powder

plastic wrap

tape

1. Spread a handful of sand, pebbles, and stones evenly across the bottom of a cake pan. Using your notebook and pencil, sketch the location of the stones and pebbles.

2. Prop up one end of the pan on a stack of books about 3 inches (7.5 cm) high.

3. Pour both bottles of glue into a bowl. Fill the empty glue bottles about half full with warm water. Shake the bottles well and then empty the bottles into the bowl.

4. Stir the glue mixture with a spoon.

5. Measure ½ cup (120 mL) warm water into the other mixing bowl. Add 1 teaspoon (5 grams) borax powder. Stir together with the other spoon.

6. Pour the water and borax mixture into the bowl with the glue.

Ever-changing Earth

The planet we live on is constantly changing. The changes aren't always abrupt or powerful. Drops of water, invisible gases, and underground plate movement are all causes of Earth's various changes. Look around you. You can see changes happening all over! These changes are fundamental for life on Earth.

7. Stir about 10 times until a lumpy mixture begins to form. Quickly remove the lump, stretch it out, and place it along the upright end of the cake pan. The mixture should be runny and wet.

8. Tightly cover the pan with plastic wrap. To make the pan airtight, tape down the edges of the plastic wrap.

9. Observe the glacier periodically for several hours. Leave it overnight. Frequently compare it to your sketch. How has the landscape changed? Does your glacier push some rocks and sand into piles?

Glossary

atmosphere (AT-muh-sfeer)—the mixture of gases that surrounds Earth

biology (bye-OL-uh-jee)—having to do with plant and animal life

carbon dioxide (KAHR-buhn dy-AHK-syd)—colorless, odorless gas that people and animals breathe out

erosion (i-ROH-zhuhn)—the wearing away of land by water or wind

glacier (GLAY-shur)—a huge moving body of ice found in mountain valleys or polar regions

infrared rays (in-fruh-RED RAYZ)—heat rays; a form of radiation similar to visible light that is given off by all warm objects

landscape (LAND-skape)—the form of the land in a particular area

lava (LAH-vuh)—the hot, liquid rock that pours out of a volcano when it erupts; lava is magma that reaches Earth's surface

magma (MAG-muh)—melted rock found beneath the surface of Earth

mantle (MAN-tuhl)—the layer of hot rock that surrounds Earth's core

molten (MOHLT-uhn)—melted by heat; lava is molten rock

plate tectonics (PLAYT tek-TONN-iks)—the scientific theory that the Earth's surface is made of large plates that move very slowly

sediment (SED-uh-muhnt)—tiny bits of rock, shells, plants, sand, and minerals that settle to the bottom of a liquid

tsunami (tsoo-NAH-mee)—a large, destructive wave caused by an underwater earthquake or volcano

vegetation (vej-uh-TAY-shuhn)—plant life or the plants that cover an area

weathering (WETH-ur-ing)—breaking down of solid rock into smaller and smaller pieces by wind, water, glaciers, or plant roots

Read More

Anderson, Michael. *Investigating Plate Tectonics, Earthquakes, and Volcanoes.* Introduction to Earth Science. New York: Rosen Educational Services, 2012.

Chambers, Catherine. *Are Humans Damaging the Atmosphere?* Earth Debates. Chicago: Capstone Heinemann Library, 2015.

Gosman, Gillian. *What Do You Know About Plate Tectonics?* 20 Questions: Earth Science. New York: PowerKids Press, 2014.

Throp, Claire. *Journey to the Center of the Earth.* Fantasy Science Field Trips. Chicago: Capstone Raintree, 2014.

Internet Sites

FactHound offers a safe, fun way to find Internet sites related to this book. All of the sites on FactHound have been researched by our staff.

Here's all you do:
Visit *www.facthound.com*
Type in this code: **9781491448151**

Check out projects, games and lots more at
www.capstonekids.com

Index

Appalachian Mountains, 20
atmosphere, 22

carbon dioxide, 25
cooling, 25
core, 4
crust, 4, 6

earthquakes, 4, 6, 11, 14
erosion, 16, 19

freezing, 20

gases, 10, 22, 25, 29
glaciers, 4, 26, 27, 29
greenhouse effect, 22, 23

heating, 4, 22, 23, 25

infrared rays, 22
islands, 7

lava, 8, 9, 10

magma, 6, 8, 10, 11
mantle, 4
melting, 4, 26
Mount St. Helens, 10
Mount Tambora, 13

Niijima, 7

Pangaea, 9
plate tectonics, 6, 8, 9, 11, 28

rivers, 16, 19

scientists, 9, 25
shorelines, 4, 14, 16

thawing, 20
tsunamis, 6, 14, 16

volcanoes, 4, 6, 7, 10, 13, 14

weathering, 20
Wegener, Alfred, 9